The Description Vault

A Writer's Guide to Character Description

Description Vault Collection

Ebook Version – 2nd edition

Misty Polish

The Description Vault
Cover by Misty Polish
Editing by Ashley Lavering
Formatting by Misty Polish

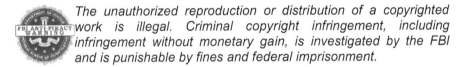
READ AT YOUR OWN RISK!

Although the author has made every effort to ensure that the information in this book was correct and accurate at press time, the author does not assume and hereby disclaim any liability to any party for any loss, damage, or disruption caused by errors or omissions, whether such errors or omissions result from negligence, accident, or any other cause. Some information in *The Description Vault* may -be inaccurate.

ISBN- 9781983058431

I want to thank you personally for picking up this book, for giving it a try, and for adding it to your collection of writing tools and reference books.

I also want to thank Ashley for being my sounding board and support. Everyone needs a cheerleader like her!

Never give up on your dreams. Write the story in your heart. Write what you want. There is no wrong story.

table of contents

introduction

The way we use words to describe our characters decides how our readers visualize what we have seen in our minds. We need to paint a clear picture of our unique characters. Don't be repetitive. Break free of those cookie cutters and dive into a deep vault of words and phrases to describe your characters.

Just like a first impression, there's only one really good shot at describing your characters. Even describing what they look like can set the mood....

Let's use an example from when Jake meets the girl of his dreams:

1st:

Jake walked into the room and saw her sitting with a group of friends. She was beautiful. Now if he could only get lucky enough to talk to her.

2nd:

Jake walked into the room. His blue eyes gazed over her slowly, taking in her tiny frame. The way her dress split high on her thigh had him lingering a bit longer. After a moment more, he fought against the fear of her rejection and walked over to her before he lost his nerve. He hoped tonight was his lucky night and she'd talk to him.

3rd:

Jake walked into the room. His gaze instantly fell on her.

The music playing softly from the stage faded as he stood there, frozen, taking in the woman who stole time. Slowly, he took in her slender frame, from her dainty ankles hidden behind black straps and the heels that barely covered her feet to her sculpted legs that had his heart hammering.

His breath caught as he dared to take in the rest of her. The slit in her red dress stopped high on her smooth bare thigh. Even from across the room, he knew his hand would fit perfectly in the curve of the small of her back, and it begged him to come closer.

Her laugh was the only thing he could now hear. The rest of the room disappeared, letting him bask in her presence.

i

She turned, just enough for Jake to see a dimple beside thin pink lips that spread wide as she smiled. High cheekbones highlighted her almond shaped, caramel colored eyes, contoured by makeup, though not heavily done like other girls he usually saw. Even her short pixie hairstyle had every strand in place with longer golden-brown wisps sweeping across her forehead.

This was the luckiest night of his life. He saw the woman of his dreams. Now, he just had to talk to her.

Each version, we can see the description grow more and more until a vision is conveyed to the reader. Let's review.

1st: We know she is beautiful, but we don't know why, so we create a personal version of her in our mind of what we *think* she looks like.

2nd: We now know she is tiny and is wearing a dress. So now, we can add that to the version we had from the 1st version.

3rd: And now, we know, she is intoxicating to Jake! We can clearly see what he sees and how it makes him feel, even though the narrator isn't talking about him. Description is HUGE!

Now think... what else could be added to the 3rd Version to dig deeper?

Usually (not always), after you meet the character you don't keep revisiting what they look like, so use this first impression to create a lasting image in your reader's mind.

This guidebook is merely a reference to make it easier for you to find words to help you create those moments for your characters. Physical appearances look different on everyone.

Author's Note:

The Description Vault is a guide for physical appearances only, not emotional or dialect. I just want to say that some words are not flattering, but they are real. They describe real features, but they are not intended to upset or offend anyone. I am not including words that lean more towards erotica to keep it clean for all readers. Also, this book is just to help get your creative juices flowing as you may come up with many different ways you want to describe your characters that aren't in this book. You are a fabulous writer after all, you make magic with words, so description is right up your alley! While this is not a dictionary, inside *The Description Vault*, you will find words that describe shape, size, color, action, names of, and synonyms for the main word. I hope you enjoy and find it useful!

~ Misty

I remember as a child hearing my grandma say things like "Ewe's not fat, ewe's fluffy!" Way to be descriptive grandma…

abdomen

Descriptive Words

Baby Belly ~ *Also called a Baby Bump. When a woman's stomach sticks out with a prominently rounded shape.*

Beefy ~ *Not fat but not muscular, however strong. Usually used with a male.*

Beer Belly ~ *A man who usually drinks beer heavily, creating a large belly that gives the appearance of a pregnant woman's belly.*

Beer Gut ~ *A very large, overhanging stomach caused by consuming an excessive amount of alcohol.*

Blubber ~ *Another term for fat or chubby.*

Bulging ~ *Protruding*

Chiseled ~ *Strong, Well-defined, Distinguished, Ripped*

Chubby ~ *Not fat, but not toned. Thick with rolls.*

Corpulent ~ *Fat, Obese, Rolls*

Enormous ~ *Exceeds the average size. Very large.*

Fat ~ *Overweight, Chubby, Heavyset*

Firm ~ *Solid*

Flabby ~ *Soft, Loose, Untoned, Sagging*

Flat ~ *Toned, Smooth*

Hairy ~ *Covered in hair.*

Hard ~ *Solid, Toned, Muscular*

Large ~ *Enormous, Exceeds the average size.*

Lean ~ *Skinny, Not fat*

Massive ~ *Large, Enormous*

Muffin Top ~ *When wearing a tight pair of jeans/pants and the belly hangs over the waistband just like a muffin top hangs over the paper.*

A Guide to Describing Your Characters

Muscular ~ *Well-defined muscles, Toned, Powerful*

Overhanging ~ *Projecting or jutting over waistband.*

Plump ~ *Chubby, Fat*

Pot Belly ~ *A protruding belly.*

Pouch ~ *Average to skinny body/build with a large stomach*

Pregnant ~ *A woman carries a baby in her womb. The longer she carries, the larger her stomach may get. Round, protruding.*

Protruding ~ *Project, Jut, Bulge, Swell, To stick out*

Pudgy ~ *Thick, Not fat but not skinny, Small rolls*

Rolls ~ *Thick, layers of fleshy mass that droop.*

Round ~ *Like a ball, Not flat*

Sculpted ~ *Chiseled, Well-defined*

Six Pack ~ *Washboard, well-defined, tight abdomen muscles that resemble a 6 pack of soda.*

Smooth ~ *Flat, Possibly toned, Not hairy*

Soft ~ *Not muscular or solid, Squishy*

Solid ~ *Firm, hard, Muscular*

Spare Tire ~ *A large roll of fat that sits around the waist.*

Taut ~ *Solid, Firm, Hard, Tense*

Toned ~ *Well-defined muscles, hard, solid*

V-Cut ~ *Well- defined group of muscles that make a V just below the abs and above the groin.*

Washboard Abs ~ *Six pack, Flat, Toned, Muscular, Lean*

Well Defined ~ *So toned that the muscle can be seen. Sharp or clearly defined.*

Action Words

Ache
Bloat
Bulge
Flex
Full
Gassy
Growl
Gurgle
Nervous
Rumble
Stuffed
Suck In
Swollen
Talking ~ *When the stomach growls and gurgles, it talks.*

Synonyms

Abs
Abdomen
Belly
Gut
Middle
Midsection
Midriff
Stomach
Tummy
Waist
Waistline

Phrases

*Abs of steel ~ *Rock hard abs.*

*Butterflies in stomach ~ *when someone feels nervous or excited, they might feel a flutter that is described as butterflies*

*Carries their food storage with them ~ *Large, fat, or pot belly.*

*Looks nine months pregnant ~ *Someone who is not pregnant, but has a round protruding belly that resembles a pregnant swollen belly of nine months.*

*She has a bun in the oven ~ *Baby bump. A woman who is pregnant and is starting to show.*

ankle

Descriptive Words

Boney ~ *Very skinny, Thin, Can see the bone*

Cankles ~ *Cankles are when the calf tapers down and meets the foot abruptly, almost giving the allusion of no ankles. Cankles are only used as a description for females. Also described as thick or fat ankles.*

Chunky ~ *Thick, Solid, Cankles*

Contorted ~ *Twisted, Bent in an abnormal shape*

Dainty ~ *Small, Delicate, Pretty, Feminine*

Delicate ~ *Easily broken, Dainty, Frail, Thin, Feminine*

Fat ~ *Thick, Chubby, Round*

Knobbly ~ *Knotted, Twisted, Contorted, Distorted, Bones stick out making it appear knobbly*

Narrow ~ *Long, Slender, Thin*

Petite ~ *Small, Delicate, Pretty, Feminine*

Slender ~ *Thin, Possibly weak, Slight.*

Thick ~ *Wide, Fat*

Weak ~ *Frail, Thin, Small, Delicate, Dainty, Easily broken*

Wide ~ *Thick, Fat.*

Action Words
Crack
Pop
Roll
Swollen

Synonyms
Anklebone
Joint
Tarsus

Honorable Mention closely related to ankle...
Heel

arm

Descriptive Words

Bare ~ *Uncovered*

Cannons ~ *Large, Powerful, muscular*

Exposed ~ *Uncovered, Naked, bare*

Shredded ~ *Well-defined muscles, Toned*

Hairy ~ *Covered in hair.*

Lanky ~ *Long, Skinny, Dangling arms*

Long ~ *Lanky, Not short*

Massive ~ *Large, Enormous, Powerful*

Muscular ~ *Well-defined muscles, Powerful, Toned*

Naked ~ *Bare, Exposed, No clothing, Uncovered*

Powerful ~ *Strong, Muscular.*

Protective ~ *Strong, Powerful, Muscular*
In romance, arms can give a feeling of security and protectiveness.

Puny ~ *Lanky, Weak, Smaller than average*

Scrawny ~ *Thin, Lean, Lanky, Skinny.*

Sculpted ~ *Chiseled, Well-defined muscles*

Short ~ *Not long, Small*

Stiff ~ *Rigid, Hard to bend*
usually from old age or injury.

Strong ~ *Powerful, Muscular, Robust*

Stub ~ *When a partial or whole arm is amputated, or a person is born without it, it leaves a small "stub". Caused from a birth defect or injury.*

Tiny ~ *Small, Puny, Smaller than average, Scrawny.*

Toned ~ *Well-defined muscles, Sculpted, Hard, Solid*

Tree Trunks ~ *Long, Massive, Powerful arms*

Twigs ~ *Small, Tiny, Puny, Scrawny*

Uncovered ~ *Bare, Naked, Exposed, No clothing*

Weak ~ *Frail, Easily broken, Thin*

Action Words
Break
Clothesline ~ *A character's arm straight out to the side, knocking his or her opponent over.*
Curl Up
Dislocate
Flex
Pull Up
Push
Rotate
Swing
Throw
Toss

Synonyms
Biceps
Forearm
Triceps
Upper Arm
Wing

Phrases
*Big Guns ~ *Large or massive biceps.*
*Farmer's Tan ~ *A distinct tan line where the arm of the t-shirt ends.*
*Spaghetti Arms ~ *Thin, lanky arms.*

beard

*Also see Mustache on page 64

Descriptive Words

Abrasive ~ *Harsh, Rough, Sandpaper-like, Scratchy*

Bristly ~ *Rough, Stiff, Prickly, Scratchy*

Bushy ~ *Thick, Shaggy, Woolly*

Coarse ~ *Rough, Abrasive, Stiff*

Curly ~ *Wavy, Corkscrew, Not straight, Kinky, Frizzy, Ringlets*

Disheveled ~ *Untidy, Unkempt, Messy*

Dreadlocks ~ *Rope-like strands, Braided, Twisted or Locked*

Forked ~ *Divided, branched, Split into two*

Full ~ *Thick, Bushy*

Long ~ *Extended, Lengthy*

Lustrous ~ *Shiny, Smooth, Thick*

Manly ~ *Male, Masculine, Male oriented, Rugged*

Masculine ~ *Manly, Male oriented, Rugged, Male, Macho.*

Matted ~ *Tangled, Unkempt, Disheveled, Ratted in a thick mass*

Messy ~ *Dirty, Unkempt, Grimy, Filthy, Uncombed*

Neat ~ *Tidy, Combed, Clean, Well groomed*

Patchy ~ *Inconsistent, Not full, Thin, Patches of hair*

Prickly ~ *Rough, Spiky, Short, Bristly, Scratchy*

Rough ~ *Bumpy, Coarse, Abrasive, Harsh, Sandpaper-like, Scratchy*

Santa Claus ~ *Long, White, Thick, Full, Lustrous*

Scraggly ~ *Thin, Unkempt, Ragged, Untidy*

Scruffy ~ *Dirty, Unkempt, Ragged, Mangy.*

Shaggy ~ *Long, Thick, Unkempt, Bushy, Woolly, Rough, Untidy*

Shiny ~ *Lustrous, Clean*

Silky ~ *Soft, Fine, Lustrous, Clean, Sleek*

Stiff ~ *Rigid, Hard, Rough, Abrasive, Coarse*

Thick ~ *Bulky, Bushy, Woolly, A lot of hair*

Thin ~ *Patchy, Not full, Fine, Sparse*

Trimmed ~ *Cut, Neatly shaven, Shaped, Tidy, Well-groomed*

Uncombed ~ *Unkempt, Untidy, Ragged, Disheveled, Messy*

Uneven ~ *Not straight, Crooked*

Unkempt ~ *Untidy, Uncombed, Dirty, Disheveled, Messy, Scruffy, Scraggly, Shaggy.*

Untrimmed ~ *Uncut*
*Although this beard may not be trimmed, it does not mean it is unkempt, an untrimmed beard can be well-maintained, or disheveled.

Wild ~ *Disheveled, Messy, Ragged, Rugged, Desolate, Unruly*

Wiry ~ *Coarse, Rough, Stiff, Bristly, Prickly, Harsh.*

Types of Beards

3-Day-Stubble ~ *Short, trimmed hair that gives the illusion of 3 days of growth. Well-maintained.*

Amish ~ *A beard with no mustache.*

Anchor ~ *A beard that traces the jawline with a small strip from chin up to bottom lip and has a mustache that is not connected.*

Balbo ~ *With no sideburns, this beard "floats" along the jawline in a neatly trimmed strip. Like the Anchor, it has a small strip from chin up to bottom lip and has mustache that is not connected.*

Chin Strap or Chin Curtain ~

This beard is connected to the sideburns and continues to circle the chin. It has no mustache.

Clean Shaven ~ *No beard or mustache.*

Circle Beard ~ *Full goatee with thick mustache. Jawline is shaved and sideburns are trimmed short.*

Ducktail ~ *A full beard that is trimmed short on the cheeks and jaw where it comes to a longer point under the chin. This beard can be worn long or short.*

Fu Manchu ~ *'Perfect for your villain'. This beard/mustache is only on the upper lip where the hair is short except at the ends, which can be grown out long. The rest of the face is clean shaven.*

Goatee ~ *This is just like a Circle Beard, however, the hair can grown as long or short as the man wants.*

Horseshoe ~ *Full mustache with the ends growing down into two bars all the way to the chin. The rest of the face is clean shaven.*

Imperial ~ *Starting at sideburns down the cheeks turning into a mustache, with no hair on chin or jaw line creates an Imperial Beard. Usually worn thick and full.*

Mutton Chops ~ *Hair starting at the sideburns going down the cheeks, no mustache, and no hair on chin.*

Scruff ~ *A couple days of growth. A stubble.*

Van Dyke ~ *Mustache with a chin beard, separated at the corners. It is a pointy beard.*

Synonyms
5 O'Clock Shadow
Facial Hair
Peach Fuzz
Scruff
Stubble
Whiskers

body shape
*Also see Build on page 14

Descriptive Words and Shapes

Apple ~ *Top heavy*

Athletic ~ *Strong, straight, Lean*

Bean Pole ~ *Tall and thin.*

Body Builder ~ *Muscular, Toned, Bulging muscles*

Curvy ~ *Small waist, Larger bust and hips, Thick, Plus size*

Dancer – Dancer's Body ~ *Strong, Lean, Long, Small, Lithe*

Fit ~ *Lean, Strong, Athletic*

Healthy ~ *Fit, Lean, Strong*

Hourglass ~ *Body makes a figure 8, Small waist with larger bust and hips*

Lean ~ *Thin, Not a lot of fat*

Lithe ~ *Dancer's Body, Flexible, Pliant, Limber.*

Muscular ~ *Toned, Strong, Well-defined muscles, Brawny, Sinewy, Strapping, Powerful, Athletic*

Obese ~ *Overweight, Heavy, Fat, Chubby*

Pear ~ *Bottom heavy, Hips and thighs are larger*

Petite ~ *Dainty, Small, Small boned, Feminine*

Plump ~ *Thick, Chunky, Not thin*

Round ~ *Wide waist and hips with narrow shoulders.*

Short ~ *Not tall, Petite.*
Short torso with long legs, or long torso with short legs.

Skinny ~ *Thin, Lean*

Slender ~ *Lean, Thin, Willowy, Graceful*

Slim ~ *Skinny, Thin, Lean*

Sporty ~ *Athletic, Well-defined, Body Builder, Muscular, Strong, Lean*

Straight ~ *Tall, Thin, Rectangle, Slightly masculine, Lacking in curves*

Stocky ~ *Large boned, Round, Bulky, Solid*

Square ~ *Boxy*
If the body is a similar size on top and bottom, it is square.

Tall ~ *Not short, Height, Towering.*

Thick ~ *Not fat or overweight, but not skinny. Curves, Healthy*

Triangle ~ *A Pear Shape, Bottom heavy*

Willowy ~ *Tall, Lean, Slender, Lithe.*

<u>Synonyms</u>
Body
Shape
Silhouette
Structure

booty

Descriptive Words

Ample ~ *Chubby, Fat, Wide, Big, Round*

Bare ~ *Naked, Uncovered, Visible, Unclothed, Showing skin*

Big ~ *Wide, Large, Round*

Bony ~ *Skinny, No fat, Flat, When sitting can feel bones*

Bubble ~ *Round, Curvy, Plump*

Cold ~ *No warmth, Freezing, Cool to touch*

Curvy ~ *Round, Bubble, Plump, Ample, Plus size*

Enormous ~ *Large, Fat, Wide, Bigger than average*

Exposed ~ *Naked, Uncovered, Visible, Showing skin*

Firm ~ *Hard, Solid, Toned, Tight*

Flabby ~ *Fat, Wide, Loose, Not toned*

Flat ~ *Not round, Lacking in curves, Bony, Straight*

Full ~ *Round, Toned, Curvy*

Hairy ~ *Covered in hair, Visible hair*

Large ~ *Wide, Round, Big, Plump*

Naked ~ *Exposed, Uncovered, Unclothed*

Nude ~ *Naked, Exposed, Uncovered*

Plump ~ *Large, Bubble, Curvy, Fat, Flabby*

Round ~ *Curvy, Big*

Saddle ~ *Wide, Large*

Sculpted ~ *Toned, Muscular, Firm*

Shaped ~ *Toned, Round, Sculpted*

Smooth ~ *Soft, Tender, Not rough*

15

Soft ~ *Smooth, Tender, Squishy*

Taut ~ *Tight, Hard, Flexed*

Thick ~ *Large, Round, Wide, Big*

Tight ~ *Firm, Hard, Solid, Toned*

Toned ~ *Sculpted, Fit, Muscular*

Uncovered ~ *Naked, Exposed, Visible, Unclothed, Showing skin*

Wide ~ *Saddle, Large, Fat, Goes out toward hips*

Action Words
Mooning
Squeeze

Synonyms
Ass
Behind
Booty
Bottom
Bum
Buns
Butt
Buttocks
Caboose
Cinnamon Buns
Derrière

Fanny
Gluteus Maximus
Hind
Hinny
Posterior
Rear
Rump
Tail
Tush

Phrases
*Junk in the Trunk ~ *Large, Wide, Saddle.*
"He/She has a lot of junk in the trunk!"
*Wide Load ~ *Saddle*
"That woman/man has a wide load!"
*Plumber's Crack ~ *When a man bends over or squats and you can see his booty crack.*

build

*Also see Body Shape on page 10

Descriptive Words

Anorexic ~ *Thin, Frail, Skeletal, Unhealthy*

Athletic ~ *Toned, Strong, Muscular, Lean*

Average ~ *Not fat but not skinny, The perfect in-between, Usually thin but not toned or muscular.*

Bean Pole ~ *Tall, Skinny, Slender, Lanky*

Beefy ~ *Burly, Hulky, Strong, Thick, Solid, Well-built, Heavy*

Broad ~ *Wide, Strong, Powerful, Heavy*

Body Builder ~ *Muscular, Toned, Bulging muscles*

Burly ~ *Strapping, Beefy, Heavy, Solid, Thick*

Dancer ~ *Strong, Lean, Long, Small, Lithe*

Frail ~ *Weak, Fragile, Small, Thin, Old*

Heavy ~ *Beefy, Solid, Thick, Husky*

Hunchback ~ *Deformed shape on back that forms a hump.*

Husky ~ *Heavy, Solid, Thick*

Lanky ~ *Slender, Tall, Long, Thin*

Large ~ *Big, Wide, Broad, Fat*

Lean ~ *Slender, Thin, Athletic, Dancer, Skinny.*

Masculine ~ *Manly, Muscular, Broad, Rugged, Burly, Husky*

Muscular ~ *Toned, Strong, Powerful, Thick, Visible muscles*

Obese ~ *Heavy, Overweight, Thick, Corpulent*

Portly ~ *Stout, Heavy, Fat, Plump*

Robust ~ *Strong, Muscular, Powerful, Rugged, Husky*

Rugged ~ *Manly, Strong, Robust, Brawny, Strapping*

Short ~ *Not tall, Small, Petite, Midget, Dwarfish*

Slender ~ *Thin, Lean, Willowy*

Slim ~ *Thin, Lean, Trim*

Slouch ~ *Slump, Hunch, Not standing up straight*

Solid ~ *Heavy, Strong, Rigid*

Strapping ~ *Robust, Rugged, Strong, Powerful, Muscular*

Stocky ~ *Thick, Chunky, Heavy, Brawny, Solid, Beefy*

Straight ~ *Lean, Trim, Lacking in curves*

Strong ~ *Powerful, Muscular, Robust, Athletic*

Stout ~ *Fat, Short, Portly, Plump*

Sumo ~ *Heavy-set, Obese, Fat, Excessive amount of body fat*

Tall ~ *Towering, Giant, All legs*

Toothpick ~ *Scrawny, Lanky, Tall, Slender, Thin, Lean*

Towering ~ *Tall, Lanky, Stands taller than average*

Wide ~ *Broad, Large, Stocky*

Synonyms
Body
Figure
Form
Frame
Height
Physique
Shape
Structure

Phrases
*All legs ~ *A woman who has long legs.*

18

cheeks

Descriptive Words

Ashen ~ *Pale, Ashy, Gray, White, Ghostly*

Baby – Baby Cheeks ~ *Fat, Plump, Puffy, Cherub, Round*

Bony ~ *Sunken, Skeletal*

Cold ~ *Devoid of warmth, Icy*

Crimson ~ *Red, Blush, Flushed, Scarlet, Ruddy.*

Dimples – Dimpled ~ *A depression in one or both cheeks when someone smiles.*

Fat ~ *Baby Cheeks, Plump, Puffy*

Freckled ~ *Dots, Speckles
Flecks of brown over cheeks and sometimes the nose.

Gaunt ~ *Lean, Bony, Sunken, Skeletal*

Hairy ~ *Covered in hair, Bearded*

Lean ~ *Thin, Gaunt, Can see the cheekbones*

Leathery ~ *Hard rough texture, Weather beaten, Wrinkled, Browned, Withered*

Pallid ~ *Pale, Pasty, White, Peaked, Ashen, Gray*

Pasty ~ *Pallid, Ashen, Gray, White, Peaked*

Peach Fuzz ~ *Sparse, light hair covering cheeks and chin. Usually on an adolescent teen boy.*

Pink ~ *Blush, Rosy*

Puffy ~ *Swollen, Plump, Fat*

Rosy ~ *Pink, Blush, Flushed, Glowing, Sunburned*

Round ~ *Round like an apple, Puffy, Plump, Cherub, Baby Cheeks*

Ruddy ~ *Red, Rosy, Crimson, Brownish-red complexion, Blush*

Shaven ~ *No hair, Clean shaven, No beard/mustache*

Smooth ~ *Soft, Silky, Velvety*

Soft ~ *Smooth, Silky, Supple*

Sunken ~ *Gaunt, Skeletal, Lean, Bony, Can see the cheekbones, Hollow*

Tanned ~ *Brownish complexion from being in the sun.*

Thin ~ *Lean, Gaunt, Bony*

Unshaven ~ *Bearded, Hairy, Peach Fuzz*

White ~ *Ashen, Pale, Gray, Ghostly, Pasty, Not tanned*

Withered ~ *Leathery, rough texture*

Action Words
Blush
Flushed
Glowing
Pale
*Color **rushing** to cheeks

chest

Descriptive Words

Bare ~ *Uncovered, Naked*

Broad ~ *Wide, Large*

Covered ~ *Clothed, Not exposed, No skin showing*

Exposed ~ *Unclothed, Skin showing*
*This can be a full exposure or partial.

Flat ~ *Lacking curves or mounds, Small, Straight*

Hairless ~ *No hair, Smooth*

Hairy ~ *Covered in hair.*

Handful ~ *A comparison of size for a woman's chest. Her breast can be measured as a handful.*

Hard ~ *Solid, Strong, Powerful, Rock hard, Tough, Muscular*

Manly ~ *Powerful, Broad, Hard, Strong*

Mound ~ *Hump, Mump.*

Muscular ~ *Strong, Powerful, Hard*

Naked ~ *Full exposure, Uncovered, Unclothed*

Perky ~ *When a woman's chest stands out. No sagging.*

Powerful ~ *Strong, Robust, Muscular*

Round ~ *Curvy*

Smooth ~ *Hairless, Soft*

Uncovered ~ *Uncovered, Naked, Exposed*

Warm ~ *Hot, Heat*

Action Words
Flex

Jerk (as with a sob)

Raise

Phrases
*Mosquito Bites ~ Very small woman's breast.

*Well Endowed ~ Very large woman's breast.

Synonyms
Boobs

Bosom

Breast

Bust

Cleavage

Hooters

Knockers

Melons

Mounds

Pecks

Rib Cage

chin

*Also see Jaw / Jawline on page 52

Descriptive Words

Angular ~ *Bony, Sharp, Pointed*

Bearded ~ *Covered in hair*
See Beard

Bony ~ *Scrawny, Sharp, Gaunt*

Chiseled ~ *Well-defined, Sculpted, Carved*

Cleft ~ *A dimple in the chin, usually in the middle.*

Dainty ~ *Small, Petite, Feminine*

Dimpled ~ *Cleft*

Double Chin ~ *Fat under the chin giving the appearance of a second chin, Chin rolls*

Hairy ~ *Covered in hair, Bearded*

Long ~ *A chin that is longer than average or juts out.*

Masculine ~ *Large, Prominent, Pronounced, Bearded, Strong*

Narrow ~ *Long, Tapered, Pointed*

Petite ~ *Dainty, Small, Feminine*

Pointed ~ *Angular, Sharp, Bony, Narrow*

Powerful ~ *Strong, Masculine, Brawny*

Prominent ~ *Obvious, Pronounced*

Pronounced ~ *Strong, Striking, Prominent.*

Protruding ~ *Sticks out, Juts out, Extended, Stands out*

Receding ~ *The chin slopes backward.*

Round ~ *Rounded chin / jaw line, Not sharp*

Sharp ~ *Angular, Pointed, Bony*

Shaven ~ *Clean shaven, No hair / beard, Smooth*

23

Smooth ~ *Soft, Silky, Shaven*

Strong ~ *Prominent, Masculine, Powerful*

Stubbly ~ *5 O'Clock shadow, Scruff, Not clean shaven, Coarse hair, Whiskered*

Square ~ *The chin has a square shape, Boxy, Not rounded or angular*

Tiny ~ *Small, Petite, Dainty.*
*A Receding Chin can also appear tiny.

Unshaven ~ *Bearded, Hairy, Stubbly, Whiskered*

Whiskered ~ *Unshaven, Stubbly, Bearded, Hairy.*
*Usually coarse hair.

Wide ~ *Not narrow or long.*

Action Words
Jut
Tremble

Synonyms
Jaw
Jawbone
Jawline
Mandible

ears

Descriptive Words

Crooked ~ *Bent, Twisted, Deformed, Not symmetrical on both sides*

Deformed ~ *Misshapen, Distorted, Bent, Crooked*

Droopy ~ *Hanging, Floppy, Dangling*

Elf / Elfin ~ *Sharp, Pointed at the top*

Elephant ~ *Wide, Large, Sticks out, Floppy*

Fairy ~ *Sharp, Pointed at the top*

Feminine ~ *Dainty, Petite, Small*

Flat ~ *Lays flat against the head.*

Floppy ~ *Droopy, Hanging*

Folded ~ *Creased, Doubled over, Bent*

Gauged ~ *Piercing with plugs.*

Hairy ~ *Hair that sticks out from the canal, or on lobe.*
*Usually, this happens a lot with old age in men.

Large ~ *Big, Elephant, Satellite*

Lobeless ~ *The ear lobe does not hang but is attached directly to the head.*

Long ~ *Hangs low, Wide, Narrow, Big*

Petite ~ *Small, Dainty, Feminine*

Pierced or Double Pierced ~ *Able to wear earrings. Holes through the earlobe. Sometimes the person has the cartilage in the top of the ear pierced as well. Modernly, the Daith Piercing is a piercing through the Crux Helix (the inner most cartilage fold on the ear).*

Pink ~ *Rosy, Flushed*

Pointy ~ *Sharp, Angular, Elf, Fairy*

Red ~ *Sunburned, Pink, Rosy, Flushed*

Round ~ *Curved, Lobeless.*

Satellite ~ *Sticks out, Wide, Large, Big*

Symmetrical ~ *The same on both sides of the head, in size, shape, and placement.*

Sharp ~ *Angular, Pointed, Elf, Fairy*

Small ~ *Dainty, Petite, Feminine*

Twisted ~ *Crooked, Bent, Distorted*

Action Words
Buzzing
Deaf
Wiggle
Ringing

Synonyms
Lobes

eyebrows

Descriptive Words

Bushy ~ *Thick, Hairy, Untrimmed*

Bushman ~ *Thick, Full, Not maintained*

Curved ~ *Shaped, Trimmed*

Microbladed ~ *Microblading is a technique of semi-permanent tattooing small lines like hairs to shape and fill in the eyebrows.*

Painted ~ *Drawn or filled in eyes brows with makeup, usually with an eyebrow pencil.*

Penciled ~ *With a makeup eyebrow pencil, the eyebrow is shaped and filled in.*

Plucked ~ *Shaped, clean, Neat *Using tweezers, the eyebrow can be **plucked** into shape.*

Pointy ~ *Some eyebrows have a natural point in the middle, and others are shaped with various ways to be shaped into a point.*

Prominent ~ *Eye catching, Noticeable, Striking, Pronounced*

Shaped ~ *Trimmed, Plucked, Microbladed, Curved, Neat*

Shaved ~ *An eyebrow might be shaved off, leaving no hair. There are also eyebrow tools to shave and shape the eyebrow.*

Slanted ~ *Sloped, Tilted, Angled*

Straight ~ *No curve, Not shaped*

Thick ~ *Bushman, Full, Wide. *Thick eyebrows can be either maintained or not, it depends on the character.*

Thin ~ *Sparse, Not a lot of hair*

Tinted ~ *A semi-permanent dye that colors, shapes, and fills in the eyebrows.*

Trimmed ~ *Shaped, Sharp lines, Maintained, Neat*

Unibrow ~ *When an eyebrow reaches across the nose touching the other one, giving the appearance of one eyebrow.*

Wild ~ *Crazy, Bushman, Not maintained, Thick, Sticking out*

Phrases
*Hidden beneath Bushman Eyebrows ~ *When eyebrows are not maintained, thick, full, and extra hairy, the eyes can be **hidden under bushman eyebrows**.*

Action Words
Arched
Bunched
Cocked
Drawn
Furrowed
Knit
Lifted
Raised

Synonyms
Brow

eyes

Descriptive Words

Bags ~ *Puffy under the eye.*

Big ~ *Wide, large.*

Bloodshot ~ *Red, tinged with blood.*

Brooding ~ *When someone is in deep thought, serious, unhappy, regret, and/or displeasure, they might have brooding eyes. Looks angry or sad.*

Closed ~ *Eyelids are closed, you cannot see the eyeball.*

Cloudy ~ *Appears white, foggy, blurred.*

Cold ~ *Stare, glare,* intently look coldly at someone. Usually associated with anger or jealousy.*

Crows Feet ~ *Fine lines around the eye. Usually appears when the person laughs or smiles.*

Dark ~ *Circles under the eyes. Bruised, black eye. Tired. Eyeliner or mascara can also run or have residue making the eye appear dark.*

Deep ~ *If there are dark circles under the eyes then they can appear deep, sunken, or hollow.*

Dilated ~ *The pupil is bigger, larger.*

Droopy ~ *Lazy Eye. When one or both eyes' upper eyelid hangs lower.*

Dull ~ *Lifeless, no shine or glisten. Cloudy.*

Empty ~ *To look or stare with flat, unemotional eyes. Haunting, hollow.*

Fiery ~ *Angry, hints of red, glare, mad. *Shooting fiery darts with her stare.*

Glassy ~ *Watery, shiny, glazed over.*

Hazy ~ *Blurred, cloudy, foggy*

29

Heated ~ *Angry, Sultry, Warm, Glare, Full of emotion*

Hollow ~ *Empty, flat. Also can look hollow with dark circles under the eyes.*

Large ~ *Big, wide.*

Lifeless ~ *Dull, no shine or glisten, empty, hollow.*

Long Lashes ~ *Thick, full lashes that extend up toward the eyebrow.*

Painted ~ *To paint the eyes means to put on makeup. *Eye shadow, eyeliner, mascara.*

Pale ~ *Light, lacking in color.*

Sad ~ *Brooding, gloomy, cheerless.*

Small ~ *Little.*

Sunken ~ *Hollow, gaunt, empty.*

Squinty ~ *Partially closed. Narrowing of the eyes to try to see something.*

Tired ~ *Dry, red, itchy, heavy.*

Watery ~ *Glossy, glassy, shiny, glazed, tears.*

Wide ~ *Large, big, set apart farther.*

Worried ~ *Concerned, Arched brow, Soul searching, Anxious, Sad*

Wrinkled ~ *Crows Feet, fine line around the eyes.*

Eye Types

Almond ~ *Oval. Cannot see white on top or bottom of iris.*

Asian ~ *Slanty. A skin fold that covers the inner angle of the eye. *Epicanthic Fold.*

Close Set ~ *Set close to the nose, they are less than one eyeball width apart.*

Downturned ~ *This shape drops at the outer corners.*

Hooded ~ *Puffy, droopy. A layer of skin droops over the crease.*

Monolid ~ *No crease, flat surface.*

Oval ~ *Almond.*

Protruding ~ *Bulging. The eyelids project from the eye socket area.*

Round ~ *You can see white on the top and bottom of the iris.*

Slanted ~ *Turned upward or downward.*

Upturned ~ *An almond shape that lifts at the end.*

Wide Set ~ *Set farther from nose, they are more than one eyeball width apart.*

Synonyms
Eyeball
Ocular
Peepers

Colors
Blue ~ Azure, Baby Blue, Cerulean, Cobalt, Cornflower, Denim, Electric, Gunmetal, Ice, Indigo, Light Blue, Midnight, Sapphire, Sky Blue,

Brown ~ Almond, Amber, Caramel, Chestnut, Chocolate, Coffee, Cognac, Golden Brown, Hazelnut, Honey, Mud, Nut, Russet Scorched Earth

Gray ~ Pearl Gray, Silver, Steel, Stormy

Green ~ Emerald, Evergreen, Forrest, Ice Green, Jade, Hazel Green, Mint, Sea Green / Seafoam, Swamp,

Hazel

Obsidian ~ Black, Ebony, Midnight

Red ~ Albino

Violet ~ Amethyst, Lavender

Action Words

Blink

Flutter

Follow

Gaze

Glance

Glare

Glimpse

Glower

Lock

Look

Narrow

Ogle

Peer

Peek

Roll

Scan

Scathing

Shoot Daggers

Soften

Sparkle

Stare

Strain

Squint

Twinkle

Watch

Wink

Phrases

*Bat your eyes ~ *Flutter, blink seductively, flirt.*

*Bedroom eyes ~ *A seductive looking glance.*

*Bug out ~ *Bulging, wide eyes, surprised, afraid.*

*Four eyes ~ *A name used for a person who wears glasses.*

*Lock eyes on ~ *To be set in a stare, Two characters stare at each other with their gaze not moving*

face

Descriptive Words

Acne Covered ~ *Pimples, Zits, Blackheads*
*Skin on face can also be oily with this, but not always.

Aglow ~ *Glowing, Shiny*

Chiseled ~ *Sculpted, Carved, Well-defined, Strong*

Clean ~ *Washed*

Complexion ~ *The texture and color of skin.*

Feminine ~ *Delicate, Soft, Pretty, Womanly*

Freckled ~
*Brown flecks on cheeks and nose.

Friendly ~ *A recognizable face of someone you know, a friend's face, comfortable. An expression of happiness, a welcome expression.*

Handsome ~ *Manly, Chiseled, Sculpted, Well-defined, Attractive*

Oily ~ *Shiny, A person with oily skin is prone to acne, Pimples, Zits, Blackheads*

Pale ~ *Ashen, Sick, White, Grave, Color drained*

Pretty ~ *Attractive*

Puckered ~ *Creased, Wrinkled, Furrowed, Lined, Drawn together*
*When a person draws or gathers their face creating wrinkles and/or folds.

Puffy ~ *Swollen, Bloated*
*This can be caused by weight gain, crying, allergies, water weight, ect...

Ruddy ~ *Red, Blush, Sunburned, Rosy, Flushed*

Sour ~ *Puckered, Squished*
Can also be an expression when someone is in a bad or **sour mood.*

Swollen ~ *Puffy, Bloated*
*This can be caused by weight gain, crying, allergies, water weight, ect...

Wrinkled ~ *Lines and creases in skin, Fine lines around eyes, Laugh lines around mouth*

Complexions

Ashen ~ *Pale, Gray, White, or Blue coloring*

Brown ~ *Light to dark brown, Tans easily, Never sunburns*

Black ~ *Dark brown to black, Tans easily, Never sunburns*

Fair ~ *White, Sunburns easily, but can get a healthy summer glow, Pale, Light*

Light ~ *Pale, Freckles, Sunburns easily (almost always), A porcelain complexion, a lot of times there are yellow or beige undertones.*

Medium ~ *Creamy white, Can get mild sunburns but tans after, Sometimes this has olive undertones*

Olive ~ *Light brown or tanned skin, Yellow, green or golden undertones, Rarely gets sunburned and tans easily*

Ruddy ~ *Red, Pale, Sunburns easily, Almost never tans*

Sallow ~ *Green (sick), Yellow*

Tan ~ *Light to dark brown, Tans easily, Rarely sunburned*

Shapes

Diamond ~ *Narrow forehead, Narrow chin, Wide cheekbones*

Heart ~ *Wide forehead, Long pointy chin / jaw line*

Long ~ *Narrow, Oblong*

Oblong ~ *Long, Narrow, Oval*

Oval ~ *Long, forehead is a touch wider than chin, Chin / jaw line is rounded.*

Round ~ *Wide cheekbones, Rounded chin, Chubby (although they can be thin)*

Square ~ *Straight, Boxy, Defined lines with jaw line*

Triangular ~ *Square chin that is wider than forehead.*

Action Words
Frown

Grimace

Screw Up

Scowl

Set *(As in your face is set into a particular expression)*

Wince

Wrinkle

Synonyms
Features

Mask

Mug

Phrases
*Angel face ~ *Looks sweet or innocent.*

*Baby face ~ *Looks young, sweet, sometimes has chubby cheeks.*

*Poker face ~ *Flat expression with no emotion. Even if the person is happy, they conceal it with their expression.*

feet

Descriptive Words

Arched ~ *When the arch of the foot is very high.*

Bare ~ *Barefoot, Uncovered, No shoes or socks*

Blistered ~ *Blisters on foot are usually caused by breaking in new shoes or walking for long amounts of time, hiking or in extreme conditions.*

Bony ~ *Can see bones, Thin, Narrow*

Callused ~ *Hard, Tough, Rough*

Club Foot ~ *Birth defect in which the foot is bent or twisted out of shape. Turned in unnaturally, Rotated inward*

Cold ~ *Lacking warmth, Freezing*

Cracked ~ *Dry, Chapped, Callused, Rough*

Dainty ~ *Small, Petite, Feminine*

Dirty ~ *Unwashed*

Dry ~ *Cracked, Callused, Rough, Chapped*

Exposed ~ *Uncovered, No shoes, Barefoot, Showing skin*

Fat ~ *Chubby*

Flat ~ *Little or no arch.*

Long ~ *Narrow, Thin*

Narrow ~ *Long, Slender*

Numb ~ *No feeling*
* Possibly from injury, fallen asleep, disease (neuropathy – in which pain, tingling and numbness occur.).

Petite ~ *Dainty, Small, Feminine*

Pigeon Toed ~ *The feet are turned inward.*

Reek ~ *Stinky, Sour, Raunchy*
*Sometimes an infection will smell horrid.

Rough ~ *Hard, Callused, Dry, Coarse*

Sandaled ~ *Barefoot in a shoe that covers mainly the bottom / sole. Straps hold the shoe in place.*

Shoed ~ *Wearing shoes, Not barefoot, Covered*

Smooth ~ *Soft, Not dry*

Socked ~ *Not wearing shoes but has socks covering the foot.*

Soft ~ *Smooth, Supple*

Stink ~ *Reek, Smells bad*

Stubby ~ *Short, Stumpy, Thick, Wide*

Swollen ~ *Puffy.*
*Possible water weight. Can be caused by standing on them all day. if a woman, she could be pregnant. Injury also can play a factor in puffy or swollen feet.

Tiny ~ *Small, Dainty, Petite*

Uncovered ~ *Naked, No shoes or socks*

Webbed ~ *When two or more toes are fused together. Birth defect.*

Wide ~ *Broad, Fat, Chubby*

Action Words
Bend
Flex
On Point
Planted
Tip Toe

Synonyms
Clodhopper
Foot
Tootsies

Honorable Mention closely related to feet...
Piggies
Toes

forehead

Descriptive Words

Broad ~ *Wide, High*

Creased ~ *Wrinkled, Furrowed*

Flat ~ *Smooth, Wide, Masculine*

High ~ *Broad, Wide, Tall*

Large ~ *Wide, Broad*

Lined ~ *Wrinkled, Creased, Worried*

Smoothed ~ *Even, Flat, No wrinkles*

Sweaty ~ *Glisten with beads of sweat.*

Uneven ~ *Wrinkled, Lined*
*Possibly the person has crooked hairline.

Wide ~ *Broad*

Wrinkled ~ *Lined, Creased, Fine lines.*
*Can come with old age.

Widow's Peak ~ *The hairline dives down in a V in center of forehead.*

Action Words
Furrowed
Lift
Scrunched ~ *Furrowed, Wrinkled, Lifted, Lined*

Synonyms
Brow
Hairline
Middle Eye

gait

Description Words

Agile ~ *Moves quick and easy, Light-footed, Lithe*

Awkward ~ *Clumsy, With difficulty, Gawky, Uncoordinated*

Bouncy ~ *Jerky, Jumpy, A little hop in their step*

Bowlegged ~ *An outward bowing at the knee with the lower leg bent inward.*

Brisk ~ *Quick, Fast, Agile, Swift*

Clumsy ~ *Awkward, Falls and trips easily, Graceless, Uncoordinated*

Confident ~ *Stands tall, Erect, Squared shoulders, Assertive, Poised, Measured, Even*

Crutch ~ *Using a crutch or crutches to help walk.*
Also can use a cane or walker. A limp may be noticeable.

Distinctive ~ *Unique, Characteristic, Individual to that person*

Drunken ~ *Stumble, Awkward, Clumsy, Stagger, Sway, Teeter, Wobble*

Fast ~ *Quick, Agile, Brisk, Swift*

Graceful ~ *Agile, Elegant, Fluid, Poised*

Halted ~ *Jerky, Limp, Coming to a stop*

Hitched ~ *Jerky, Jumpy, Bouncy, Rough, Twitchy*

Jerky ~ *Spasmodic, Twitchy, Hitched, Convulsive, Sharp movements*

Lame ~ *Unable to walk, Limp, Hobble*
Usually caused by injury or illness.

Lively ~ *Energetic, Spirited, Bouncy, Enthusiastic*

Measured ~ *Calculated, Confident, Steady, Even*

Pain-Filled ~ *Limp, Hitch, Jerky, Slow, Hobble, Lame, Rigid, Crutch*

Polished ~ *Suave, Confident*

Rhythmic ~ *Steady, Even, Measured, Unfaltering*

Rigid ~ *Stiff, Unbending, Awkward, Jerky, Inflexible*

Scissor Gait ~ *Rigid*
*Flexed at the knee as if crouching, the thighs can touch or sometimes cross like scissors. This is usually a gait associated with Cerebral Palsy.

Slow ~ *Steady, Measured, Sluggish, Even*

Sluggish ~ *Slow, Listless*

Smooth ~ *Fluid, Steady, Effortless*

Stagger ~ *Sway, Teeter, Wobble, Walk unsteady, Drunken*

Stiff ~ *Rigid, Inflexible, Unable to move easily*

Stilted ~ *Stiff, Awkward, Wooden*

Stumble ~ *Loss of balance, Slip, Trip, Fall*

Teeter ~ *Sway from side to side or front to back, Unsteady, Stagger, Stumble*

Unbending ~ *Stiff, Rigid, Inflexible*

Uneven ~ *Rough, Jerky, Hitched, Not smooth, Possible limp*

Unstable ~ *Wobbly, Unsteady, Shaky*

Unsteady ~ *Wobbly, Shaky, Sway, Teeter*

Wobbly ~ *Sway from side to side, Unsteady, Unstable, Sway, Teeter*

Action Words

Amble

Follow

High Step

Hobble

Limp

March

Pace

Run

Saunter

Shuffle

Skip

Stagger

Stroll

Stumble

Swagger

Sway

Tip Toe

Traipse

Tramp

Tread

Waddle

Walk

Synonyms

Carriage

Pace

Stance

Step

Stride

Walk

Phrases

*Light on their feet ~ *Walks lightly or softly. Tip-toe.*

*Two left feet ~ *Clumsy, awkward.*

hair

Descriptive Words

Bald ~ *Having little to no hair, Hairless, Smooth, Shaven*
*Can be caused by hair loss or purposely shaved.

Bleached ~ *Whitened either by bleach, dye, peroxide, or sun. Light blonde or white.*

Braided ~ *Three strands of hair intertwined, Weaved, Plaited*

Brittle ~ *Frail, Weak, Split ends, Breaks off easily*

Coarse ~ *Thick, Strong*

Crimped ~ *Wavy, Crinkled*

Curly ~ *Ringlets, Corkscrews, Kinky, Permed*

Dirty ~ *Not washed, Greasy, Oily, Grimy*

Disarray ~ *Messy, Tangled, Disheveled, Not in place*

Disheveled ~ *Disarray, Messy, Not in place, Tangled, Knotty, Wild, Windblown*

Dry ~ *Frizzy, Dull, Listless*

Dyed ~ *Colored, Tinted, Highlighted*
*Can be any color or a mix of colors.

Dull ~ *Listless, Dry, Lackluster, Washed out, Dingy*

Fine ~ *Thin, Light, Wispy, Flyaway*

Flat-Ironed ~ *When a straightener or flat-iron is used, the hair becomes soft, smooth, straight.*

Frizzy ~ *Dry, Damaged, Crinkly, Kinky*

Gleaming ~ *Healthy, Shiny, Glowing, Lustrous*

Greasy ~ *Oily, Grimy, Dirty, Shiny*

Kinky ~ *Crimped, Corkscrew, Tight curls, Wild*

A Guide to Describing Your Characters

Lackluster ~ *Dull, Lifeless, Listless, Dry, Dingy*

Long ~ *For women long hair is usually any length past the shoulders and past the ears for men *however it can also be described as long for a man if it hits the shoulders and medium at the ears. This will be a writer's discretion.*

Lustrous ~ *Shiny, Glossy, Healthy, Bouncy, Radiant*

Matted ~ *Tangled, Mass of knotted hair, Uncombed, Unkempt, Disheveled*

Oily ~ *Greasy, Grimy, Dirty, Shiny*

Permed ~ *Curls, Ringlets, Spiral, Kinky, Crimped*
Permed hair is hair that has been processed with chemicals and rods to give a semi-permanent curl to the hair.

Radiant ~ *Lustrous, Healthy, Shiny, Glowing*

Receding ~ *When hair stops growing along the forehead and temples, the hairline goes back higher above the forehead.*

Shaggy ~ *Bushy, Thick, Uncombed, Disheveled, Messy*

Shiny ~ *Healthy, Lustrous, May have a sheen, Greasy, Oily*

Short ~ *For women short hair is up by her chin and shorter, for men it is anything shorter than their ears.*

Silky ~ *Soft, Smooth, Healthy, Lustrous, Shiny*

Sleek ~ *Smooth, Glossy, Lustrous, Silky*

Soft ~ *Smooth, Silky*

Straight ~ *Without curls or waves. This can be natural or with a straightener.*

Tangled ~ *Matted, Ratted, Uncombed, Messy*

Thick ~ *Full, Coarse*

Thin ~ *Wispy, Sparse, Receding*

Tousled ~ *Untidy, Disheveled, Windblown, Messy*

Uncombed ~ *Messy, Tangled*

Unkempt ~ *Messy, Straggly, Bedraggled, Uncombed*

Unruly ~ *Wild, Unmanageable, Distracting*

Untidy ~ *Messy, Wild, Tangled, Matted, Bedraggled, Windblown*

Wavy ~ *Curled, Kinky*
*This can be natural, processed, or had a tool such as a curling iron used to achieve this look.

Wild ~ *Disarray, Unruly, Messy, Unmanageable*

Windblown ~ *Messy hair caused from the wind blowing through it, Tangled*

Wispy ~ *Thin, Fine, Soft, Flowy*

Colors

Auburn ~ *Burnt Earth, Copper, Ginger, Golden Brown, Red, Reddish Brown, Reddish-Blond, Rust*

Black ~ *Ebony, Inky, Jet, Midnight, Raven.*

*Blonde (*Female*)

*Blond (*Male, unisex, unknown sex*) ~ *Bleached, Champagne, Dirty, Fair, Flaxen, Golden, Light, Sandy, Strawberry, Sun-Dipped, Tawny, Towhead, Yellow*

Brown ~ *Amber, Auburn, Bronze, Brunette, Caramel, Chestnut, Chocolate, Cinnamon, Coffee, Mahogany, Russet, Tan, Tawny, Toffee*

Gray ~ *Ash, Silver, Smokey, Steel*

Red ~ *Burgundy, Carrot, Cherry, Crimson, Fiery, Flaming, Scarlet, Strawberry*

Salt and Pepper (Mix of white and black hair colors)

White ~ *Alabaster, Bleached, Frosted, Snowy, Ice, Crystal*

Hairstyles (*NOTE* There are so many styles out there it would be hard to name them all, below are the most common or well known)

A-Line ~ *Is shorter in the back near the nape then angles longer in the front.*

Afro ~ *An African hairstyle that has grown out without straightening or ironing.*

Asymmetrical ~ *Longer on one side.*

Bangs ~ *A blunt cut of hair across the forehead.*

Beach Waves ~ *Tousled waves.*

Beehive ~ *Teasing of hair with hairspray on top of head to get a lift and shape that resembles a beehive.*

Blow Out ~ *With a round brush, hair is dried from roots out with a dryer.*

Bobcut ~ *A blunt cut above the shoulders.*

Bowl Cut ~ *A bowl is placed on the head and then trimmed around the bowl.*

Braid ~ *Also known as Plaits or Plaited. Usually three strands of hair that is braided together with medium to long hair.*

Bun ~ *Hair is pulled back into a knot.*

Butch ~ *Hair on top is short and then tapers down.*

Buzzcut ~ *A cut made with razors. Butch, crew, flat top, ect...*

Chignon ~ *A twisted bun pinned at the nape of the neck.*

Cornrows ~ *Braided hair in a series of locks close to the head.*

Comb Over ~ *Hair combed over from the part, usually to cover a bald spot.*

Crewcut ~ *Hair on top of head is short with it longer in front and shortest at the crown, then tapers down the sides.*

Cropped ~ *A short hairstyle cut short and close to the head, but long enough to have a fringe.*

Dreadlocks ~ *Sections of hair that has been backcombed, teased, or hand rolled, locked at the roots.*

Ducktail ~ *Hair combed back from sides, overlapping to look like a ducktail in the back, with a pompadour on top in the front.*

Fade ~ *Short, tapered hair.*

Fauxhawk ~ *A fake Mohawk. The sides are not shaved, but the top can mimic a Mohawk, sometimes it is a purposely messy look.*

Feathered ~ *Layered hair that is brushed back, giving the appearance of feathers.*

Fishtail ~ *A braid that looks like a fish bone.*

Flattop ~ *A crew cut where the top is cut flat.*

Flipped ~ *The ends of the hair are curled to flip up.*

French Braid ~ *A braid that looks like it is braided into the hair. Also can be inside out, creating a Dutch Braid.*

French Twist ~ *The hair is gather at the back of the head and twisted up into a sort of bun.*

Mohawk ~ *Shaved on the sides leaving a strip of short, medium, or long hair down the middle. The person can use products to help make the middle strip stand up like a fan.*

Mullet ~ *Short in the front, long in the back.*

Pageboy ~ *A long bob.*

Permed ~ *Chemically processed to make the hair have a semi-permanent curl.*

Pigtails ~ *Shorter hair is placed into one or more sections and placed in a ponytail with a curl in the ends*

Pixie ~ *A short wispy woman's haircut.*

Pompadour ~ *Hair is pushed back off and high over the forehead.*

Ponytail ~ *Long hair that is pulled back and secured by a hair tie or rubberband.*

Rattail ~ *Shaved head except for a long piece in the back which is braided tightly down the back.*

Razorcut ~ *Short choppy layers.*

Shag ~ *Full, thick, choppy layers.*

Spiky ~ *Hair that sticks up all over. Some may only have it stick up on the top.*

Undercut ~ *The sides and back are cut short or shaved while the top is longer, overlapping the short sides and back.*

Updo ~ *When a woman wears her hair up.*

Action Words

Blowing *in the wind*

Brushed

Fell *it fell in waves over her shoulders*

Flowy

Swinging *hair in a ponytail can swing*

Tangled

Tickled *if it falls and touches skin it can tickle*

Synonyms

Curls

Locks

Mane

Tresses

hands

Descriptive Words

Able ~ *Skillful, Strong*

Arthritic ~ *Inflammation of the joints can cause swelling and pain.*

Bony ~ *Thin, Frail, Gnarled*

Calloused ~ *Hard, Rough, Thick*
*A man who works hard with his hands may have calloused palms.

Capable ~ *Able, Skilled, Experienced*

Contorted ~ *Twisted, Gnarled, Warped, Buckled, Deformed*

Delicate ~ *Frail, Petite, Womanly, Dainty*

Double Jointed ~ *Unusually flexible joints.*

Experienced ~ *Skillful, Capable, Able, Expert*

Expert ~ *Skilled, Experienced, Capable, Adept*

Fat ~ *Chubby, Thick, Large, Meaty*

Frail ~ *Delicate, Petite, Small, Weak, Dainty, Thin, Easily broken, Old*

Flexible ~ *Moves easily, Pliable, Bendable*

Gentle ~ *Soft, Caring, Tender, Compassionate*

Gnarled ~ *Knobbly, Rough, Twisted, Bumpy*

Knobbly ~ *A bony, gnarled, lumpy appearance.*

Rough ~ *Calloused, Hard, Rugged, Chapped*

Powerful ~ *Strong, Muscular, Manly*

Skilled ~ *Capable, Expert, Experienced*

Soft ~ *Gentle, Caring, Tender, Compassionate, Smooth, Supple*

Strong ~ *Powerful, Muscular, Tough, Forceful*

Stubby ~ *Short, Fat, Chubby*

Warm ~ *Hot*

Weak ~ *Frail, Delicate, Dainty, Petite*

Wide ~ *Manly, Strong, Large.*

Action Words
Balled
Caress
Clap
Clasped
Cupped
Extended
Fisted
Flexed
Fold
Handshake
Hit
Jazz Hands
Offered
Proffered
Punch
Shake
Snap
Spirit Fingers
Steepled
Stroked
Wave
Outstretched

Synonyms
Fist
Grip
Palm

Honorable mention closely related to the hand...
Fingers ~ *Digits, Middle Finger, Pinky, Pointer, Ring Finger, Sausages, Thumb, Index*

*Fingers can be long, narrow, slender, stubby, short, fat, thin, nimble, double jointed, strong, weak, swollen, arthritic.

hips

Descriptive Words

Ample ~ *Full, Bountiful, Large, Full-figure*

Bearing ~ *Wide, Full, Curvy*

Big ~ *Large, Full, Plus size*

Bony ~ *The hip bone sticks out. Thin, Skinny, Lean, Skeletal*

Broad ~ *Wide*

Curvy ~ *Full, Thick, Plus size, Rounded, Voluptuous*

Fat ~ *Chubby, Wide, Large, Obese, Big*

Feminine ~ *Curvy, Child bearing, Thick*

Full ~ *Thick, Curvy, Wide*

Narrow ~ *Straight, Lean, Athletic*

Round ~ *Curvy*

Shapely ~ *Attractive, Pleasing, Rounded, Curvy*

Straight ~ *Narrow, Lean, Athletic*

Seductive ~ *Tempting, Attractive, Provocative, Alluring, Curvy, Thick, Voluptuous*

Thick ~ *Chunky, Chubby, Full, Wide*

Voluptuous ~ *Curvy, Shapely, Ample, Full-figured, Plus size*

Wide ~ *Broad*

Womanly ~ *Curvy, Child bearing, Voluptuous, Shapely*

Action Words

Jiggle

Rock

Sashay

Shake

Sway

Swing

Synonyms

Side

Phrases

*Child Bearing ~ *Hips wide enough to deliver a baby. Wide.*

jaw / jawline
*Also see Chin on page 20

Descriptive Words

Angular ~ *Bony, Sharp, Pointed*

Bearded ~ *Covered in hair. See Beard.*

Chiseled ~ *Well-defined, Sculpted, Carved*

Cleft ~ *A dimple in the chin, usually in the middle.*

Dainty ~ *Small, Petite, Feminine*

Dimpled ~ *Cleft*

Hairy ~ *Covered in hair, Bearded*

Long ~ *A chin that is longer than average or juts out.*

Masculine ~ *Large, Prominent, Pronounced, Bearded, Strong*

Narrow ~ *Long, Tapered, Pointed*

Petite ~ *Dainty, Small, Feminine*

Pointed ~ *Angular, Sharp, Bony, Narrow*

Powerful ~ *Strong, Masculine, Brawny*

Prominent ~ *Obvious, Pronounced*

Pronounced ~ *Strong, Striking, Prominent*

Protruding ~ *Sticks out, Juts out, Extended, Stands out*

Receding ~ *The chin slopes backward.*

Round ~ *Rounded chin / jaw line, Not sharp*

Sharp ~ *Angular, Pointed, Bony*

Shaven ~ *Clean shaven, no hair / beard, Smooth*

Smooth ~ *Soft, Silky, Shaven*

Strong ~ *Prominent, Masculine, Powerful*

Stubbly ~ *5 O'Clock shadow, Scruff, Not clean shaven, Coarse hair, Whiskered*

Square ~ *The chin has a square shape, Boxy, Not rounded or angular*

Tiny ~ *Small, Petite, Dainty.*
*A Receding Chin can also appear tiny.

Unshaven ~ *Bearded, Hairy, Stubbly, Whiskered*

Whiskered ~ *Unshaven, Stubbly, Bearded, Hairy.*
*Usually coarse hair.

Wide ~ *Not narrow or long.*

Action Words
Clench
Jut
Slack
Unhinged

Synonyms
Chin
Jawbone
Mandible

laugh

Laughter is expressed in different ways and is unique to each person. No laugh sounds the same. While laughter can't be seen, the actions it causes can be, so it earned a spot in The Description Vault.

Descriptive Words

(These words are a mix of some of the descriptions, sounds, and emotions that may trigger laughter)

Amused ~ *Delighted, elated*

Bark ~ *A laugh that coughs like a bark.*

Bitter ~ *Angry*

Boisterous ~ *Noisy, Loud, Over excited*

Booming ~ *Deep, Loud, Thunderous*

Bubbly ~ *Cheerful, Light hearted, Exuberant*

Cheerful ~ *Happy, Bubbly, Gleeful*

Cruel ~ *Bitter, Angry, Maniacal, Malicious*

Cynical ~ *Skeptical, Doubtful*

Deep ~ *Booming, Thunderous*

Faint ~ *Weak, Soft, Quiet, Muffled*

Gentle ~ *Kind, Tender, Soft, Quiet*

Hearty ~ *Booming, Deep, Boisterous*

High-Pitched ~ *Shrill, Piercing*

Hoarse ~ *Croaky, Gruff, Gravelly, Husky, Throaty, Guttural*

Hysterical ~ *Hilarious, Side splitting, Amusing*

Infectious ~ *Catching, Contagious*

Jittery ~ *Nervous*

Jolly ~ *Cheerful, Happy, Bubbly*

Jovial ~ *Cheerful, Jolly, Happy, Bubbly, Exuberant*

A Guide to Describing Your Characters

Kind ~ *Gentle*

Light ~ *Soft, Gentle, Low, Melodious*

Light Hearted ~ *Cheerful, Happy, Humorous*

Lilt ~ *Cadence, Melodious*

Loud ~ *Boisterous, Deep, Noisy, Thunderous*

Malicious ~ *Spiteful, Mean, Nasty, Cruel, Wicked*

Merry ~ *Happy, Jolly, Bubbly*

Mocking ~ *Sarcastic, Making fun of, Fake, Repeating*

Muffled ~ *Quiet, Stifled, Soft, Subdued, Hushed*

Musical ~ *Melodious, Light, Harmonious*

Nervous ~ *Worried, Anxious, Tense, Uneasy*

Pitched ~ *The sound or tone of one's voice.*

Pleasant ~ *Soft, Pleasing, Friendly, Cheerful*

Rich ~ *Deep, Strong*

Sarcastic ~ *Mocking, Cynical*

Sardonic ~ *Mocking, Sarcastic, Derisive*

Shrill ~ *High-pitched, Sharp, Piercing, Trill, Shriek*

Snort ~ *Grunt*

Soft ~ *Gentle, Sweet, Light*

Sweet ~ *Gentle, Syrupy, Charming*

Tinkling ~ *Chime*

Uneasy ~ *Nervous, Troubled, Tense*

Quiet ~ *Soft, Gentle, Light, Hushed, Muffled*

Wicked ~ *Evil, Malicious*

Synonyms

Bark

Cackle

Chortle

Chuckle

Giggle

Grin

Guffaw

Howl

Roar

Shriek

Smile

Smirk

Snicker

Snigger

Tittering

Phrases

*Crack up ~ *To laugh over something funny.*

*Die laughing ~ *Can't stop laughing, completely helpless.*

*In stitches ~ *Sides hurt after laughing for so long.*

*Knee slapping ~ *A chuckle or laugh that causes you to slap your knee.*

*Rolling ~ *Can't stop laughing, figuratively rolling on the floor.*

*Side splitting ~ **In stitches.*

legs

For this part of The Description Vault, legs consist of thighs, knees, and calves

Descriptive Words

Athletic ~ *Lean, Muscular, Strong*

Bare ~ *Uncovered, Skin showing, Naked*

Bony ~ *Scrawny, Skinny, Skeletal*

Bowed ~ *The lower leg is angled or bowed outward.*

Bowlegged ~ *An outward bowing at the knee with the lower leg bent inward.*

Bristly ~ *Rough, Stiff, Prickly, Scratchy, Not shaved*

Curvy ~ *Ample, Full, Thick*

Dimpled Knees ~ *Small depression(s) in the knee giving the appearance of dimples.*

Double Jointed ~ *Unusually flexible joints.*

Exposed ~ *Uncovered, Skin showing, Bare*

Fat ~ *Chubby, Overweight, Plus size, Thick*

Flabby ~ *Loose skin, Sagging, Soft, Not toned*

Flexible ~ *Lithe, Bendable, Stretches farther than average*

Jelly ~ *Weak, Trembling, Wobbly, Tired, Shaky*

Hairy ~ *Covered in hair, Not shaved*

Knobbly ~ *Bony, Lumpy, Bumpy *Knobbly knees.*

Lean ~ *Thin, Athletic, Sinewy, Slender*

Long ~ *Lengthy*

Muscular ~ *Strong, Powerful, Sinewy, Beefy, Strapping, Burly*

Naked ~ *Exposed, Unclothed, Uncovered, Bare, Showing the entire leg*

Prickly ~ *Rough, Stiff, Scratchy, Bristly, Not shaved*

Powerful ~ *Strong, Muscular, Athletic*

Rubbery ~ *Weak, Jelly, Wobbly, Shaky*

Shaven ~ *Not hairy, A razor is used to remove hair, Smooth*

Short ~ *Small, Little, Petite*

Sinewy ~ *Lean, Strong, Muscular*

Slender ~ *Lean, Skinny, Willowy*

Skinny ~ *Toothpicks, Slim, Scrawny, Skeletal*

Slim ~ *Slender, Thin, Lean*

Smooth ~ *Soft, Velvety, Silky*

Stocky ~ *Thick, Chunky, Solid, Powerful*

Stilts ~ *Stiff. A pair of wooden slats used to help a person walk higher.*

Strong ~ *Powerful, Muscular, Tough, Solid, Robust*

Stubby ~ *Short, Thick, Stumpy*

Swollen ~ *Inflamed, Bloated, Puffy.*
*Can be caused by water weight, being overweight, standing on legs too long, injury, ect...

Thick ~ *Chunky, Solid, Powerful, Fat, Curvy*

Thin ~ *Lean, Small, Slim, Skinny*

Toothpicks ~ *Skeletal, Very scrawny legs*

Unshaven ~ *Hairy, Covered in hair.*
*Could be just a day or two from the last shave making them prickly and scratchy.

Varicose Veins ~ *Gnarled, Large, Bulging veins that stick out*

Weak ~ *Tremble, Shaky, Jelly, Tired*

Action Words

Quaking
Shaky
Steady
Sturdy
Tremble
Unsteady
Wobbly

Tap
Trample
Trudge
Walk
Walk Lamely

Actions That Use Legs

Amble
Crawl
Creep Dance
Dart
Dash
Drag
Hobble
Jog
Leap
Limp
March
Kick
Pace
Run
Saunter
Scurry
Shuffle
Slide
Sprint
Stagger
Stamp
Stomp
Stroll

Synonyms

Appendages
Limb

Phrases

*Chicken legs ~ *Very skinny, bony legs.*

*Legs that go on for days ~ *Long, attractive legs on a woman.*

lips

Descriptive Words

Chapped ~ *Dry, Cracked, Chafe, Rough, Split*

Cleft ~ *A split in the upper lip. Can be on one or both sides of the middle.*

Closed ~ *Lips touching, not open.*

Cracked ~ *Chapped, Dry, Split*

Dry ~ *Parched, Needing moisture*

Full ~ *Plump*
The lower lip is usually larger than the top.

Hitched ~ *Tugged, Lifted or pulled upward*

Kissable ~ *Attractive, Soft, Smooth, Gentle*

Laugh Lines ~ *Fine lines that curve around the corners of the mouth.*

Open ~ *Parted, Gapping, Lips not touching*

Painted ~ *Has lipstick on lips.*

Parched ~ *Dry, Chapped, Needing moisture*

Plump ~ *Full, Big*

Pressed ~ *Lips are closed together tightly, or pushed up next to something tightly, kissing.*
She pressed her lips against his.

Sensual ~ *Attractive, Soft, Gentle, Kissable, Voluptuous*

Split ~ *Cracked, Parched, Chapped, Dry*

Swollen ~ *Plump, Puffy*

Thin ~ *Slight, Fine, Narrow*

Upturned ~ *Frown, Curve down*

Voluptuous ~ *Shapely, Ample, Full, Plump, Sensual*

Wide ~ *Full, Broad*

Action Words
Bite your lip
Lick your lips
Suck your lip
Close
Curl
Curved
Frown
Grin
Kiss
Open
Parted
Pout
Pucker
Pursed
Smile

Colors
Blue
Pink
Purple
Red ~ Crimson, Ruby

Synonyms
Chops
Kisser
Mouth

Honorable Mention closely related to lips and mouth...
Teeth ~ *Braces, Bright, Buck Teeth, Chipped, Crooked, Decayed, Gap, Missing, Retainer, Rotten, Straight, White, Yellow*

mustache
*Also see Beard on page 7

Descriptive Words

Abrasive ~ *Harsh, Rough, Sandpaper-like, Scratchy*

Bristly ~ *Rough, Stiff, Prickly, Scratchy*

Bushy ~ *Thick, Shaggy, Woolly*

Coarse ~ *Rough, Abrasive, Stiff*

Forked ~ *Divided, Branched, Split into two*

Full ~ *Thick, Bushy*

Long ~ *Extended, Lengthy*

Manly ~ *Male, Masculine, Male oriented, Rugged*

Masculine ~ *Manly, Male oriented, Rugged, Male, Macho.*

Neat ~ *Tidy, Combed, Clean, Well groomed*

Patchy ~ *Inconsistent, Not full, Thin, Patches of hair*

Prickly ~ *Rough, Spiky, Short, Bristly, Scratchy*

Rough ~ *Bumpy, Coarse, Abrasive, Harsh, Sandpaper-like, Scratchy*

Stiff ~ *Rigid, Hard, Rough, Abrasive, Coarse*

Thick ~ *Bulky, Bushy, Woolly, A lot of hair*

Thin ~ *Patchy, Not full, Fine, Sparse*

Trimmed ~ *Cut, Neatly shaven, Shape, Tidy, Well-groomed*

Uneven ~ *Not straight, Crooked*

Unkempt ~ *Untidy, Uncombed, Dirty, Disheveled, Messy, Scruffy, Scraggly, Shaggy*

Untrimmed ~ *Uncut*

*Although this beard may not be trimmed, it does not mean it is unkempt, an untrimmed beard can be well-maintained, or disheveled.

Wiry ~ *Coarse, Rough, Stiff, Bristly, Prickly, Harsh.*

Types of Mustaches

(This is not an extensive list and only the most common mustaches are listed)

3-Day-Stubble ~ *Short, trimmed hair that gives the illusion of 3 days of growth. Well-maintained.*

Chevron ~ *Wide, thick, covers the complete upper lip.*

Dali ~ *Long, narrow and thin. The ends are long and pointy.*

Fu Manchu ~ *'Perfect for your villain'. This beard/mustache is only on the upper lip where the hair is short except at the ends, which can be grown out long. The rest of the face is clean shaven.*

Handlebar ~ *Bushy and thick mustache that comes out to pointy ends.*

Horseshoe ~ *Full mustache with the ends growing down into two bars all the way to the chin. The rest of the face is clean shaven.*

Lampshade ~ *Cropped close to the upper lip, it is not longer than the lip but does go the full length of the lip. Thick, bushy.*

Pencil ~ *Trimmed very close to follow along the upper lip, looking like it was drawn.*

Pyramid ~ *Wide at the base narrowing at the nose.*

Toothbrush ~ *Most recognizable as the mustache that Adolf Hitler, Charlie Chapin, and Michael Jordan wore. A thick mustache where the hair is only in the middle of the upper lip.*

Synonyms
Facial Hair
Stashe
Stubble
Whiskers

nails

Descriptive Words

Acrylic ~ *Fake nails that are over your natural nail, Manicured*

Brittle ~ *Weak, Breaks easily, Frail.*

Blunt ~ *Trimmed flat, Straight*

Broken ~ *Chipped, Ripped*

Colored ~ *Painted, Shellacked, Acrylic, Gel*

Daggers ~ *Sharp, Pointy, Long*

Fake ~ *Not the natural nail* **Acrylic and gel are the most common fake nail, manicured.*

Flaky ~ *Brittle, Chipped*

Flat ~ *Blunt, Trimmed, Straight, No curve*

Gel ~ *Fake nails over the natural nail, Manicured*

Hangnail ~ *Ripped or torn skin around the edge of the fingernail.*

Ingrown ~ *A side of the nail grows down in the bed of the nail. Painful, can cause swelling, redness, puffiness, infection.*

Long ~ *Not trimmed short.*

Manicured ~ *Trimmed, Well taken care of, Filed, Buffed*

Painted ~ *Colored, Shellacked, Polished*

Pointed ~ *Sharp, Cat-like, Daggers, Pointy*

Polished ~ *Shellacked, Painted, Colored*

Sharp ~ *Pointy, Daggers, Pointy*

Short ~ *Trimmed short, Not grown out*

Split ~ *Chipped, Broken, Flaky*

Square ~ *Filed to a blunt flat top/end.*

Trimmed ~ *Cut, Clipped, Filed*

Untrimmed ~ *Not manicured, Untidy, Hangnails, Not clipped or cut*

Synonyms
Claws

neck

Descriptive Words

Bare ~ *Exposed, Uncovered, Naked, Nothing on or around the neck*

Beautiful ~ *Pretty, Attractive, Feminine*

Beefy ~ *Thick, Big, Brawny*

Elongated ~ *Stretched, Extended*

Exposed ~ *Bare, Uncovered, Naked, Showing skin*

Fat ~ *Chubby, Beefy, Thick, Neck rolls*

Feminine ~ *Graceful, Long, Willowy*

Graceful ~ *Swan-like, Willowy, Sensual, Slender*

Long ~ *Extended, Lengthy, Stretched*

Manly ~ *Muscular, Strong, Strapping, Thick, Sinewy*

Masculine ~ *Strapping, Manly, Strong*

Muscular ~ *Strong, Powerful, Thick, Bulging, Tough*

Naked ~ *Exposed, Uncovered, Bare*

Pretty ~ *Feminine, Attractive, Beautiful*

Sinewy ~ *Large, Thick, Muscular, Lean, Strong, Strapping*

Slender ~ *Thin, Long*

Stiff ~ *Rigid, Strong, Tense*

Stretched ~ *Extended, Elongated*

Strong ~ *Powerful, Muscular, Tough*

Swan ~ *Agile, Graceful, Long, Thin*

Swollen ~ *Puffy, Enlarged, Bloated, Thick*

Thick ~ *Large, Beefy, Strapping, Muscular*

Willowy ~ *Graceful, Thin, Slender, Agile*

<u>Honorable Mention closely related to neck...</u>

Adam's Apple

<u>Synonyms</u>

Collar

Throat

nose

Descriptive Words

Aquiline ~ *Hooked or curved like an eagle.*

Blunt ~ *Stubby, Flat or rounded tip*

Broad ~ *Wide, Blunt, Noticeable*

Broken ~ *Smashed, Swollen, Crooked*

Crooked ~ *Awkward, Deformed, Not straight, Bowed, Bent*

Curved ~ *Hooked, Aquiline*

Flat ~ *Blunt, Wide*

Freckled ~ *Brown flecks over the nose and cheeks.*

Handsome ~ *Strong, Straight, Prominent*

Hooked ~ *Curved, Aquiline, Hawk-like*

Long ~ *Narrow, Sloped*

Narrow ~ *Long, Thin, Straight*

Pig-like ~ *Wide, large, upturned nostrils.*

Pointy ~ *Sharp, Sticks out to a point*

Prominent ~ *Distinguished, Pronounced, Striking, Strong, Distinct*

Sharp ~ *Hooked, Carved, Curved, Pointy, Aquiline*

Slanted ~ *Crooked, Broken, Bowed*

Sloping ~ *Long narrow slant from bridge down.*

Smashed ~ *Broken, Shattered, Flat*

Straight ~ *Long, Narrow, Not crooked or bent*

Striking ~ *Prominent, Handsome, Distinguished*

Strong ~ *Prominent, Straight, Distinguished*

73

Tapered ~ *Sloping down from bridge.*

Wide ~ *Fat, Broad, Blunt*

Types of noses
*Remember, no two noses are alike, you can even mix and match!

Bulbous ~ *Fleshy, round, protruding.*
*See Fleshy

Bumpy ~ *Prominent curves and dips with a bumpy outline.*

Button ~ *Small, tiny dainty, round.*

Combo ~ *A mix of two different shapes/types. Example: Roman with a Bump.*

East Asian ~ *Slim, flat with shirt tip.*

Fleshy *aka Einstein ~ *Bulbous, protruding, round, fat.*

Greek ~ *Straight, sculpted, chiseled, no bumps or curves.*

Hawk *aka Beak ~ *Aquiline, hooked or curved like an eagle.*

Nixon ~ *Straight bridge with a wide tip. *Named after President Nixon, as he had this nose.*

Nubian ~ *Long bridge with a wide base. Most common in African descent.*

Roman ~ *Like a Greek nose, sculpted but with a slight bend or curve.*

Snub *aka Mirren ~ *Thin, pointy, with a slight slope up at the tip.*

Turned-Up *aka The Celestial Nose ~ *Small nose with a depression in the middle of the bridge and a protruding tip.*

Synonyms
Nostrils
Schnoz
Sniffer
Snout

74

shoulders

Descriptive Words

Bare ~ *Uncovered, Naked*

Big ~ *Broad, Wide*

Bony ~ *Can see the bones, Thin, Skeletal*

Broad ~ *Wide, Muscular, Powerful, Brawny*

Bulky ~ *Fat, Chubby, Muscular, Wide*

Burly ~ *Strong, Robust, Beefy, Strapping*

Dislocated ~ *Out of place, Out of joint, Dislodged*

Droopy ~ *Hanging, Sagging, Limp*

Exposed *~Naked, Uncovered, Bare*

Hunched ~ *Arched, Bent over, Raise the shoulders and bend over*

Large ~ *Wide, Broad, Bulky*

Muscular ~ *Strong, Broad, Powerful, Brawny*

Narrow ~ *Thin, Slender, Slight, Slim*

Padded ~ *Some sports require shoulder pads as part of their uniforms for safety, like football. Some clothing has stuffed padding in the shoulder area giving a more broad look to the wearer.*

Scrawny ~ *Skinny, Bony, Skeletal*

Strapping ~ *Burly, Robust, Strong*

Strong ~ *Tough, Powerful, Muscular*

Tense ~ *Tight, Taut, Stiff, Rigid*

Wide ~ *Broad, Large*

Action Words

Fall

Hunch

Raise

Roll

Slouch

skin

Descriptive Words

Acne ~ *Pimples, Blackheads, Red bumps, Zits*

Age Spots ~ *Brown or black flecks on the skin that come with age.*

Bare ~ *Exposed, Naked, Uncovered*

Birthmark ~ *Irregularity on the skin that shows at / or soon after birth.*

Blackened ~ *Burned, Injured, Areas of dead skin*

Blisters ~ *An abscess on the skin that is filled with fluid.*

Bruised ~ *Discolored, Black, Purple, Yellow, Green, Injury*

Bumpy *aka Chicken Skin ~ *Rough patches.*

Burned ~ *Blackened, Red, Blisters, Peeling, Damaged, Injury*

Callused ~ *Hard, Thick*

Chapped ~ *Dry, Cracked, Chafe, Raw*

Clammy ~ *Damp, Sticky, Cool, Slimy*

Clean ~ *Washed*

Cold ~ *Chilly, Frigid, Icy, Freezing, Shivering, Sick*

Cut ~ *Gash, Laceration, Slit, Wound, Injury, Stitches, Band-Aid*

Creamy ~ *Soft, Supple, Velvety*

Dead ~ *Dry, Blackened, Peeling*

Dirty ~ *Not washed.*

Dry ~ *Cracked, Chafe, Rough*

Eczema ~ *Red, scaly rash.*

Exposed ~ *Bare, Naked, Uncovered*

Flawless ~ *Smooth, No imperfections, Unblemished*

Goosebumps*aka Goose Pimples or Goose Skin ~ *The hair on the skin stands up, creating small bumps all over.*

Greasy ~ *Oily, Shiny*

Grimy ~ *Dirty, Filthy, Caked in dirt*

Hairless ~ *No hair, Smooth, Shaved*

Hairy ~ *Covered in hair, Not shaved*

Hot ~ *Fever, Flushed, Sweaty, Warm*

Itchy ~ *Scratchy, Tickly, Irritated*

Leathery ~ *Hard, rough texture. Weather beaten, Wrinkled, Browned, Withered*

Moles ~ *Brown, Tan, Black raised layers of skin cells, Bumps*

Naked ~ *Bare, Exposed, Uncovered, Showing all your skin*

Nude ~ *Wearing no clothes, Naked*

Oily ~ *Greasy, Shiny*

Powdery ~ *Covered in powder, Makeup, White*

Psoriasis ~ *Dry, itchy, scaly patches.*

Rough ~ *Dry, Chapped, Callused*

Sags ~ *Hangs, Loose, Droopy*

Scaly ~ *Flaky, Rough, Dry, Dead*

Scarred ~ *Disfigured, Wounded, Injury, Mark, Blemish*

Shiny ~ *Oily, Greasy, Wet*

Silky ~ *Smooth, Soft*

Skin Tags ~ *Short pieces of skin that grows out.*

Sliced ~ *Cut, Slit, Wound*

Smooth ~ *Soft, Silky, Velvety*

Soft ~ *Silky, Smooth*

Spider Veins ~ *Clusters of blood vessels close to the surface of the skin.*

Sticky ~ *Clammy, Warm, Tacky*

Sunburned ~ *When the sun burns the skin after too much exposure. Red, Burned*

Supple ~ *Lithe, Pliable, Limber, Flexible*

Sweaty ~ *Clammy, Damp, Sticky, Beads of sweat coming out of pores*

Tough ~ *Thick, Callused, Rough*

Uncovered ~ *Exposed, Bare, Naked*

Uneven ~ *Irregular patches and spots of darker skin.*

Varicose Veins ~ *Gnarled, large, bulging veins that stick out.*

Velvety ~ *Soft, Smooth, Silky*

Welts ~ *Red, swollen mark left on skin by a blow. Swelling, Bump*

Wrinkles ~ *Lines and creases in skin. Fine lines around eyes. Laugh lines around mouth.*

Skin Colors
Albino
Almond
Ashen
Beige
Black
Blue
Bronze
Brown
Buff
Burnt
Caramel
Chestnut
Dark
Espresso
Fair
Flushed
Golden
Honey
Ivory
Light
Natural
Nude
Olive
Pale
Pink
Porcelain
Red
Sand
Tanned
Vanilla
White

Undertones
Cool
Golden
Green
Neutral
Olive
Warm
Yellow

Complexions
Ashen ~ *Pale, gray, white, or blue coloring.*

Brown ~ *Light to dark brown, tans easily, never sunburns.*

Black ~ *Dark brown to black, tans easily, never sunburns.*

Fair ~ *White, sunburns easily, but can get a healthy summer glow.*

Light ~ *Pale, freckles, sunburns easily (almost always), this is a porcelain complexion, a lot of times there are yellow or beige undertones.*

Medium ~ *Creamy white, can get mild sunburns but tans after, sometimes this has olive undertones.*

Olive ~ *Light brown or tanned skin. Has yellow, green or golden undertones, rarely gets sunburned and tans easily,*

Ruddy ~ *Red, pale, sunburns easily, almost never tans.*

Sallow ~ *Green (sick), yellow.*

Tan ~ *Light to dark brown, tans easily, rarely sunburned.*

Synonyms
Epidermis
Hide

smile

Types of Smiles

Accepting ~ *Welcoming, friendly, Soft*

Alluring ~ *Charming, Attractive, Tempting*

Amused ~ *Pleased, Entertained, Tickled*

Arrogant ~ *Conceited, Bigheaded, Haughty*

Attractive ~ *Eye-catching, Gorgeous, Pleasing.*

Bewitching ~ *Enchanted, Entranced, Captivated*

Big ~ *Wide*

Bitter ~ *Resentful, Angry, Offended*

Brief ~ *Quick*

Bright ~ *Cheerful, Happy, Upbeat*

Brilliant ~ *Radiant, Intense, Dazzling*

Broad ~ *Wide*

Captivating ~ *Entrancing, Enchanted, Bewitched*

Charismatic ~ *Compelling, Magnetic, Alluring*

Charming ~ *Delightful, Pleasant, Charismatic*

Cheerful ~ *Happy, Lively, Jolly*

Cocky ~ *Arrogant, Smug, Overconfident*

Cold ~ *Bitter, Resentful, Vicious*

Condescending ~ *Patronizing, Arrogant, Haughty*

Confident ~ *Self-assured, Poised, Have no doubts*

Crooked ~ *Twisted, Curved, Not straight*

Dazzling ~ *Stunning, Alluring, Brilliant*

Disarming ~ Charming, Captivating, Beguiling

Embarrassed ~ Uncomfortable, Humiliated, Mortified, Self-conscious

Enchanting ~ Charming, Captivating, Enthralling

Encouraging ~ Cheering, Hopeful, To give confidence

Faint ~ Slight, A hint of a smile

Fake ~ Forged, Phony, Mocking

Fixed ~ Forced, Flat, Rigid

Fleeting ~ Brief, Short-lived, Passing

Forced ~ Strained, Unnatural, Obligatory

Friendly ~ Welcoming, Pleasant, Happy

Gentle ~ Welcoming, Soft, Friendly, Not flashy, Comforting

Genuine ~ Real, Sincere, Authentic

Goofy ~ Silly, Fun, Exuberant

Grim ~ Bleak, Uninviting, Depressing

Half ~ Not full, partial.

Hesitant ~ Weary, Unsure, Fake

Icy ~ Cold, unfriendly, hostile.

Incredulous ~ Skeptical, Doubtful

Insecure ~ Lacking in confidence, Shaky, Unsteady

Kind ~ Welcoming, Friendly, Caring

Little ~ Half, not full.

Magnetic ~ Compelling, Captivating, Alluring

Mesmerizing ~ Captivating, Exciting, Compelling

Mischievous ~ Playful, Teasing, Naughty

Mocking ~ Fake, Sarcastic, Scoffing

Nervous ~ *Anxious, Worried, Tense*

Phony ~ *Fake, Mocking, Not genuine*

Playful ~ *Silly, Friendly, Flirty, Happy*

Polite ~ *Well-mannered, Respectful, Gracious*

Radiant ~ *Bright, Dazzling, Happy*

Rare ~ *Unusual, Infrequent, Scarce.*

Reassuring ~ *Comforting, Supportive, Encouraging*

Rigid ~ *Stiff, Firm, Upset, Not happy, Disapproving*

Rogue ~ *Smolder, Does not happen often, Villainous*

Sad ~ *Depressed, Distressed, Gloomy*

Sarcastic ~ *Mocking, Derisive, Scornful*

Sardonic ~ *Mocking, Cynical, Sarcastic, Scornful*

Sharp ~ *Quick, Sour, Precise*

Sheepish ~ *Embarrassed, Guilty, Ashamed*

Shy ~ *Withdrawn, Reserved, Small*

Sinister ~ *Menacing, Threatening, Evil*

Slight ~ *Small, not full.*

Slow ~ *Long lasting, Measured, Lingering*

Sly ~ *Cunning, Teasing, Rogue, Covert*

Smolder ~ *Slow, Charming, Handsome, Use the eyes to smile*

Smug ~ *Arrogant, Conceited, Haughty*

Soft ~ *Gentle, Kind, Pleasant*

Sophisticated ~ *Polished, Customer-service smile, Refined, Elegant, Smooth*

Sour ~ *Bitter, Resentful, Angry*

Seductive ~ *Flirtatious, Alluring, Tempting, Provocative*

Sweet ~ *Soft, Kind, Pleasant*

Sympathetic ~ *Understanding, Compassionate, Supportive*

Tight ~ *Tense, Firm, Taut, Fixed*

Toothless ~ *Smiling with no teeth.*
*A baby has a great toothless smile.

Toothy ~ *Full smile showing teeth.*

Warm ~ *Friendly, Kind, Affectionate*

Weak ~ *Brief, Faint, Barely a smile*

Welcoming ~ *Friendly, Warm, Inviting*

Wisp ~ *Soft, Faint, Fleeting, Small*

Wistful ~ *Reflective, Sad, Longing*

Wry ~ *Dry, Sarcastic, Cynical*

Action Words

*(Many of the words above can also be used as an action, as **smile** is already an action, BUT it can be seen so it earned a spot in The Description Vault)*

Blazed
Flashed
Flickered
Gleamed
Sparkled
Twinkled

Synonyms

Beam
Grin
Smirk

voice

While you cannot see your character's voice, it can be heard. It may not be a physical appearance, but it earned a spot in The Description Vault.

Descriptive Words

Accent ~ *A character who speaks with a different dialect, language, or slang/terms.*
*American, English, Scottish, Australian, Southern, Eastern, Western, Ect...

Authoritative ~ *Confident, Respected, Firm*

Booming ~ *Loud, Deep, Thunderous*

Breathy ~ *An audible breathing sound, Raspy*

Broken ~ *Cracking, Changing*

Calm ~ *Steady, Fixed, Soft*

Chirpy ~ *Cheerful, Happy*

Choked ~ *Not full sound, broken.*

Clear ~ *Full sound, Strong, Unbroken*

Cold ~ *Uncaring, Unfeeling, Detached*

Composed ~ *Calm, Collected, Steady*

Confident ~ *Sure, Calm, Composed, Strong, Possible authority*

Croaky ~ *Deep, Hoarse, Froggy*

Deep ~ *Resonate, Low, Booming, Rich*

Faint ~ *Soft, Weak, Whisper*

Female ~ *Women have a higher pitch than men, usually not low or deep.*

Firm ~ *A fixed, flat tone. Steady, Calm, Authoritative*

Flat ~ *Monotone, Uncaring, Steady*

Gentle ~ *Soft, Caring, Calm, Quiet*

85

A Guide to Describing Your Characters

Grating ~ *Raspy, Annoying, Irritating, Harsh*

Gravelly ~ *Gruff, Hoarse, Raspy, Croaky*

Gruff ~ *Husky, Gravelly, Thick, Throaty*

Guttural ~ *Rough, Throaty, Deep*

High-Pitched ~ *Sharp, Shrill, High*

Hoarse ~ *Croaky, Rough, Raspy*

Honeyed ~ *Smooth, Syrupy, Sweet, Flattering*

Hushed ~ *Quiet, Soft, Low*

Husky ~ *Gravelly, Deep, Rough, Guttural*

Inviting ~ *Friendly, Pleasing, Alluring*

Loud ~ *Booming, Deep, Thunderous*

Low ~ *Soft, Soothing, Quiet, Gentle, Subtle*

Male ~ *Deep and low. Men usually do not have a high-pitched voice.*

Melodious ~ *Sweet, Pleasant, Musical*

Monotone ~ *Flat, not changing.*

Muffled ~ *Quiet, Muted, Hushed*

Musical ~ *Melodious, Sweet, Sing-song*

Nasally ~ *Breathy*
*When a person is congested and they talk, it is Nasally.

Quiet ~ *Soft, Silence, No sound*

Pitched ~ *High or low, It is the tone of the voice*

Pleasant ~ *Friendly, Agreeable, Enjoyable*

Powerful ~ *Authoritative, Booming, Strong*

Raspy ~ *Hoarse, Rough, Gruff*

Rich ~ *Deep, Strong, Powerful*

Rough ~ *Gruff, Deep, Throaty*

Shrill ~ *Piercing, High-pitched, Screech*

Singsong ~ *Melodious, Lyrical, Musical*

Sleepy ~ *Raspy, Deep, Smokey, Attractive*

Smokey ~ *Deep, Rich, Husky*

Soft ~ *Quiet, Silky, Gentle, Hushed*

Squeaky ~ *Shrill, High-pitched, Sharp*

Steady ~ *Calm, Collected, Confident*

Stern ~ *Firm, Strict, Unyielding, Serious*

Strained ~ *Broken, Weak, Cracking, Choked*

Sultry ~ *Passionate, Sensual, Thick, Honeyed*

Sweet ~ *Pleasant, Rich, Melodious, Soothing*

Thick ~ *Rich, Deep, Husky*

Throaty ~ *Husky, Deep, Low, Gruff*

Tight ~ *Firm, Unwavering, Tense*

Warm ~ *Honeyed, Low, Dark, Breathy*

Wavering ~ *Hesitant, Shy, Timid*

Weak ~ *Faint, Low, Soft*

Wheezy ~ *Breathless, Gasping, Winded, Breathy*

Whiny ~ *Shrill, High-pitched, Annoying*

Voice Type

Alto

Baritone

Bass

Soprano

Tenor

Synonyms

Sound

Speech

Tone

Action Words

Chat

Chatter

Cry

Holler

Murmur

Roar

Scream

Shout

Shriek

Sigh

Talk

Utter

Whisper

Yell

M.R. Polish has been writing since she was a young girl. She would tell her stories to anyone who would listen until she discovered she could put them onto paper.

Out on the ocean is her favorite place to be and would live on a cruise ship if she could, traveling the world, but alas, adulting and responsibilities keep her grounded.

M.R. is happily married to someone who would gladly follow her onto a ship and sail away. They have four kids, who might be more adventurous jet-setters than their mother.

"Life is too short to stand by and watch everyone else live your dreams. The bigger the dream, the bigger the adventure!" ~ M.R. Polish

You can contact M.R. Polish here:

Website: www.mrpolishauthor.com

Facebook Page: www.facebook.com/m.r.polish.author

And... it's new for me, but it's about to get fun... TikTok: www.tiktok.com/@m.r.polish

Amazon: https://www.amazon.com/M-R-Polish/e/B00AS0TWQK

(I'm on other platforms but... not as much so this is your best shot at finding me!)

References:

www.urbandictionary.com

www.dictionary.com

www.thesaurus.com

www.en.wikipedia.org

Printed in Great Britain
by Amazon

16750969R00061